A Manual of Sorrento and Inlaid Work for Amateurs, With Original Designs

A MANUAL OF
SORRENTO AND INLAID WORK

FOR AMATEURS,

WITH ORIGINAL DESIGNS.

BY

ARTHUR HOPE.

CHICAGO:
JOHN WILKINSON, PUBLISHER.
1876.

COPYRIGHT, 1876,
BY JOHN WILKINSON

KNIGHT & LEONARD, PRINTERS, CHICAGO

PREFACE

IT is now twenty years since the author of this book began his first rude attempts at scroll-sawing, with a roughly whittled saw-frame, fitted with a blade made from a watch-spring, its teeth, few and far between, unevenly and laboriously cut with a common file Since then he has watched the growth of the art in this country, stimulated by the introduction of curious and beautiful articles of fret-cutting from Germany, and inlaid work from France and Italy, and the gradual improvement in hand-saw frames, and blades of wondrous delicacy. Within the past four years, aided much by the invention of treadle machines of great simplicity and beauty, a scroll-sawing fever has swept over the country, absorbing the attention of the young and old. It would perhaps be impossible to name a village, however small, where the fever had not made its appearance. In many of our large cities scroll-sawing is taught by experienced instructors, either in classes or in private lessons.

There are many difficulties that beset the beginner; he buys worthless tools, and can do nothing with them; or imagines it is necessary to buy some expensive outfit that exceeds his means; he tries to polish and makes a botch of it, his wood warps, and obstinately refuses to be straight; his saws break, and he cannot account for it; his gluing doesn't hold together;

PREFACE.

and he imagines that inlaying can only be done by the experienced artisan. To help all such, to show them just how everything in the scroll-sawing line is done, to make everything clear so that children can teach themselves, to show ladies how they can beautify their homes, to tell those with scanty means how few tools are necessary; and, lastly, to give them some few simple, and it is hoped tasteful, designs, is the object of this book. How far he falls short of this his readers can judge for themselves.

ARTHUR HOPE.

New York, November, 1876.

CONTENTS.

Chapter		
I	Woods,	7
II	Preparation of Woods,	10
III.	Applying the Design,	13
IV	Tools,	14
V	Making a Bracket,	19
VI	Making an Easel,	22
VII	Sandpaper,	24
VIII	Glue, Shellac, Oil and Polish,	26
IX	Glued Veneers,	31
X	Overlaying,	33
XI	Inlaying,	35
XII	Silhouettes,	41
XIII	Description of Designs,	44

CHAPTER I.

WOODS

SPANISH cedar, red cedar, white holly, black walnut, satin, tulip, ebony, bird's-eye maple, rosewood, mahogany, are the ordinary and most desirable woods for scroll-sawing

SPANISH CEDAR is an excellent wood for the amateur to begin sawing with, being soft and easily worked Cigar boxes are generally made of this wood, and will furnish all the small pieces needed, at little or no expense. The old boxes should be carefully taken apart, and the pieces soaked in a basin of water. After several minutes' immersion the paper can be easily scraped off, when the wood should be placed on end to dry, which it will do without warping When quite dry, the wood can be smoothed with sandpaper (see chapter on "Sandpaper"). Very pretty brackets, easels, frames or boxes can be made of this cedar.

RED CEDAR, on account of its fragrance, is a pleasant wood to saw, and should be about three-sixteenths or a quarter inch in thickness. It is, however, very liable to split or crack, and though not a hard wood, rather hard to saw. It does well for brackets and easels.

WHITE HOLLY is a fine, close-grained wood, very easy to saw, and a universal favorite. It is used in all thicknesses from a veneer (about one thirty-second of an inch) to a quarter inch, and can be very highly polished. For all small articles, such as card-baskets, small frames, etc , a thickness of about one-sixteenth inch or a trifle more is preferable One-eighth inch holly does well for small easels, brackets, frames, paper-knives and small wall pockets; while for larger things, such as easels and brackets intended to support some weight, a thickness of three-sixteenths or one-quarter inch should be used As holly shows dirt easily, it is best before beginning to saw it, when it is not to be polished, to give it a coat of bleached shellac. For the manner of using shellac the reader is referred to the chapter on "Glues, Shellac, etc."

BLACK WALNUT is more used than any other wood, is cheap and easy to saw. All kinds of useful and ornamental articles are made from this wood. In buying it, care should be taken to select that which is of a uniform shade and free from streaks, unless for some work, an inlaid panel for instance, a piece with light streaks should be wanted. It is seldom used thinner than one-eighth inch. Brackets and easels should be made of three-sixteenths or one-quarter when they are to support any weight.

MAHOGANY is a hard, close-grained wood, easy to saw, and suitable for nearly all articles One-eighth is the ordinary thickness, though it is frequently used one-sixteenth and three-sixteenths. Before making brackets, easels and other open-work things this wood should be polished It should be remarked here that not a little of the wood commonly sold as mahogany is really a species of cedar.

ROSEWOOD has a close grain, takes a fine polish, and is difficult to saw. In working it the saw blade should occasionally be touched with a drop of oil (raw linseed or olive), as the saw frequently encounters hard, gummy places, in which, if not oiled, to allow it to slip easily, the saw is apt to break. One eighth, three-sixteenths and one-quarter inch are the ordinary thicknesses.

SATINWOOD is hard and close grained, yellowish color, somewhat oily and is very easily polished. It does well for all kinds of open and inlaid work. The dust is quite fragrant, and where worked in large quantities is said to be injurious to health; but there is no danger in using it for ordinary amateur work. Wreaths and scroll work for overlaying on picture frames are very beautiful, and when so used the thickness should not be over one-sixteenth inch. For easels, brackets, etc., it should be one-eighth or three-sixteenths.

TULIP is a finer and closer grained wood, reddish color and usually streaked. It is excellent for paper-knives and easels, and takes a fine polish. It is rather expensive, and is commonly used either in veneers or one-eighth inch.

BIRD'S-EYE MAPLE is another close-grained wood, somewhat gritty in sawing, and very beautiful when polished. It is, however, more difficult to polish than many other woods, as it requires so much filling. It answers excellently for backgrounds for silhouettes

EBONY is a very hard and heavy, close-grained wood, nearly black in color. It is one of the most expensive woods used in scroll-sawing. To saw it easily, the saw-blade should be oiled occasionally, especially where the wood is one-eighth inch or more in thickness. This is an excellent wood for paper-knives and silhouettes, and for inlaying. It is susceptible of a very high polish. A very beautiful effect can be produced by inlaying ivory in ebony, and the reverse.

CHAPTER II.

PREPARATION OF WOODS

BEFORE attempting to saw anything, care should be taken to select a good piece of wood. If the work to be done is delicate, avoid using any wood with knots, lest they should cause a break in some fragile point. The wood must also be smoothed before sawing, as it is difficult to smooth or polish open work nicely, on account of the danger of breaking. Most of the woods commonly used can be procured with a smooth finish, though they are rather expensive. In many of the large cities there are dealers who keep fine woods for sale, either sawed or planed. When the sawed woods are used, they need to be first scraped with a small rectangular piece of steel called a scraper, and afterward rubbed smooth with sandpaper. The use of glass for scraping is not advised, as it is very apt to scratch and spoil the wood. If a quantity of wood needs this scraping it will save the amateur a good deal of hard work if he lets some careful carpenter do this for him. Soft woods, such as cedar, poplar, etc., can be planed smooth enough by hand,— but all hard woods must be scraped, or rubbed down with sandpaper. The planed woods that are kept for sale usually require sandpapering to make them fit for nice articles, though they will do well enough as they are for common work. If any open-work pieces are to be polished, the polishing must be done before the sawing.

Where several things are to be made at once, the pieces of wood can be fastened together outside of the pattern with brads. Do not use tacks, as they are apt to split the wood. The writer's way of fastening woods together is as follows. He cuts the pieces all of uniform size, and about one-fourth of an inch larger than 'the pattern on each side; between these he places several pieces of stiff paper cut the same size as the wood, clamps them together or lays a weight upon them, and applies some glue to the edges In a few hours the weight can be removed, and they will be found to adhere firmly. By this process smaller pieces of wood can be used than where they are nailed together. The paper placed between the woods preserves duplicates of the patterns.

For the hand-saw, not more than two thicknesses of one-eighth inch should be sawed at once, as it is quite difficult to keep the saw perpendicular, and unless the saw is held true the under piece is likely to be spoiled. With a good treadle saw, six or eight pieces of one-eighth inch can be sawed at once with ease. The writer, with his machine, a "Fleetwood,"* frequently saws more than this at once, and of thinner woods, such as veneers, thirty can be done at a time

The amateur will frequently find in buying thin woods that they are warped, and he may find it difficult to straighten them. His difficulty will vanish if he treats the wood as follows Hold the concave side for a few minutes over the steam from a boiling

---

* He also uses two other machines for different kinds of work.

tea-kettle, and then the other side over a stove; as soon as it is straight, remove from the heat, hold firmly with the hands till cold, lay it upon a smooth surface, place a weight upon it, and it will dry flat

CHAPTER III.

APPLYING THE DESIGN

THERE are several methods of applying the design to the wood, each of which has its advocates The simplest way is to paste the pattern directly on the wood. This can be done in all cases, except on polished wood or fine white wood, which might be soiled in subsequently removing the paper. After the sawing is done the paper easily comes off by moistening it.

Another way is to fasten the pattern to the wood by means of a number of small tacks driven into the parts that are to be cut away. In this case it is advisable first to paste the pattern to a thick card, the edges of which are less likely to be torn by the saw passing through. By doing this the pattern will be preserved for future use, and it will be easy to follow its edges with a sharp-pointed pencil and copy the design repeatedly.

Still another way is to place a sheet of carbon or impression paper (usually for sale at stationers') upon the wood, and over this lay the design. Then, with either a sharp-pointed stick or hard pencil, follow carefully the lines of the design, which the carbon paper will transfer to the wood. This is slow work, however, and requires nearly as much care as the sawing itself.

Where printed designs are used, always choose those printed in light colors. Black designs are objectionable, because it is difficult keeping on the line, especially when using artificial light.

CHAPTER IV.

TOOLS.

THE tools required for hand-sawing are simple and inexpensive. A saw-frame, saw-blades, a rest, a clamp-screw, an awl, or drill-stock, a file and sandpaper. Of saw-frames, the cheapest is the ordinary birch frame, twelve, fourteen or sixteen inches in length, costing about one dollar. The following cut will show the style of this frame:

Then there are rosewood frames of the same shape, costing about one dollar and twenty-five cents. These have the advantage of being stiffer than the birch frames, and have usually a better style of clamp-screw.

Another kind is the steel saw-frame.

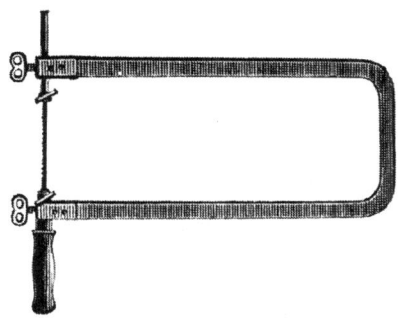

These are preferred by many because the clamp-screws are adjustable and allow the use of either a long or short saw-blade. Those who break their blades — and there are none who do not — will find great economy in using these frames, as they can save their pieces for service a second time. The steel frames cost about one dollar and a half.

Lastly, we must mention the beautiful saw-frame made by the Sorrento Wood Carving Company.

This is made of rosewood, is strong and stiff, and costs three dollars.

Saw-blades are of German, Swiss or French manufacture, and are from four and a half to five inches long. The sizes in ordinary use are —

In buying saw-blades, choose only those with sharp and regularly cut teeth. For hand-sawing, Nos. 0 and 1 are the best sizes, unless for very delicate work, when finer ones should be used. The larger blades have coarse teeth, which are liable to catch in the work and tear it. Blades of either of above sizes can be used in treadle machines, the size varying with the kind of work to be done. The best quality of saw-blades cost from fifteen to twenty cents per dozen; poor blades, for half the money.

The rest is a plain piece of inch pine about twenty inches long by six wide, with a V-shaped opening at one end.

In using the rest, the saw should always be kept near the bottom of the V, where the work will be firmly supported on both sides. This rest, if bought, should not cost over ten or fifteen cents. It is to be placed upon the table or bench with the V part projecting, and should be held in position by means of a clamp-screw.

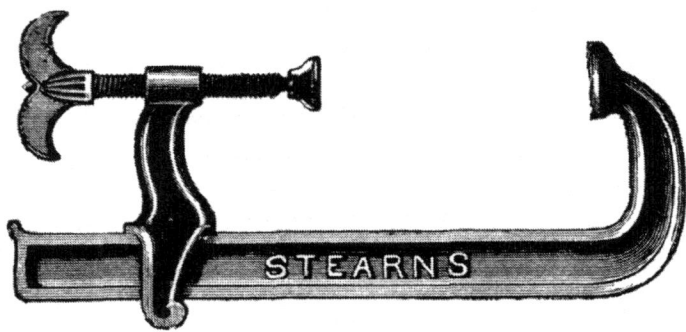

The above represents a cabinet-maker's clamp-screw, of malleable iron, and adjustable. This is decidedly better than the common cast-iron screws, which break easily, and is usually for sale at hardware stores. One opening three inches costs about thirty-five cents. These clamp-screws will be found especially useful in gluing veneers or thicker woods together.

For all open work it is necessary to have something to punch holes to let the saw-blade inside, and for single thicknesses of wood a common brad-awl, costing about ten cents, is sufficient. But where several pieces are to be sawed at once, or for delicate work or brittle wood, a drill stock is essential. The most serviceable article of this kind is a small drill stock of German manufacture, like the cut below, which is generally sold, with six drill points,

for about one dollar and twenty-five cents. It is easier to drill true with these than with those that are worked by a cog-wheel.

Next, one or more files are necessary, to finish the edges after the saw has done its work. A round file four inches long, a half-round file from two to four inches, and a flat file the same length, will answer for all fine work, and will cost from fifteen to twenty-five cents each.

Finally, an assortment of sandpaper is needed, which will be more fully described in the chapter on that subject.

TREADLE SAWS

By all means, where the amateur can afford the expense, a treadle saw should be procured. The better class will do the most delicate work, can be run with great ease, and will cut from eight to twenty or thirty pieces at a time,— the number varying of course with the thickness of the wood,— and leave the edges of the work perfectly smooth, so that a file is seldom required. There are many treadle machines in market, differing in quality as well as price. It would obviously be improper in a work of this kind to advocate any particular machine. There are few that have not some good points about them. Advertisements of various machines will doubtless appear at the end of this book, and to them the reader's attention is directed.

In using treadle machines the saw-blades should be inserted with the teeth pointing downward and toward the operator. The wood should be guided by the fingers, while the wrists rest firmly on the edges of the table. Always keep the running parts of the machine clean and well oiled, for, with proper care, one should last a lifetime.

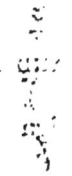

CHAPTER V.

MAKING A BRACKET

AS a first lesson, the amateur should take a piece of cigar-box wood, or any other thin wood that may be at hand, and mark thereon a series of straight and curved lines. Then lay the wood on the rest, holding it down with the left hand, fasten a No. 1 blade in the frame, and begin sawing, being careful to keep on the line. Work the frame firmly and always in one direction, keeping the blade perpendicular, and turn the wood that the saw may follow the pattern. After the motion of the saw is learned, and the beginner can saw straight or follow a curve, let him mark on his wood several Vs and squares. To saw the V, begin at the upper end and saw down to the point; then back the saw out and saw from the other end down to the point If the line is carefully followed, this will leave a sharp, clean cut angle at the point. To cut out a square hole, saw down to the angle, then work the blade rapidly up and down to make a place large enough for the saw to turn in, and then turn the wood at right angles and saw along the line to the other corner, when the same operation is to be repeated. When the beginner can make straight lines and curved lines well, and cut out an angle nicely, he will be ready to commence a bracket.

Now take a piece of wood, say one-eighth thick, smooth it with sandpaper, and apply the design as before described. The acorn bracket, Plate I, at the end of this book, will serve for an example. Note this precaution,— before tracing a pattern on the wood, always study the design to see which way the grain of the wood should run; in this case it should run up and down, for if it ran across the bracket, the stems of the acorns might easily break. Mark a point on each part to be cut out, and drill holes, smoothing off the under side that the work may turn easily. As it is better to cut out the inside first, pass the blade through one of the holes and saw in the direction shown by the dotted lines. Cut the angles as sharply as possible, to save the labor of afterward finishing them with a file. In commencing at A, it will be best to saw first along the line to D; then back the saw out to A and saw along the other side of the point around to D again, when the piece will drop out And, again, in sawing around the acorn, begin at X and saw up to C, and around the stem to I, thence along the point to C, when the piece of wood will fall out, and the sawing can then proceed from the end of the pointed piece in the direction of T. In finishing the acorn, it would not do to start afterward at S and saw along toward V, as in that case, after the saw had reached V, there would be left nothing but the slender stem to support the wood, and in sawing toward X the acorn would probably break off. On the contrary, the acorn should be finished by sawing from X toward V.

When the main part of the bracket has been cut out, a semicircular piece of wood should be cut out for the shelf. Then lay the bracket upon the wood, and with a sharp pencil trace thereon either the right or left half. This is then to be sawed out in the same way as the bracket, and is for a support to the shelf. Now take a small half-round file and file all the corners true, and straighten all the edges where the saw has wandered from the line. Next, take the sandpaper block (see chapter on "Sandpaper," and with it rub the bracket carefully till all the pencil marks have disappeared. The edges on the under side will be found to be ragged, but the sandpaper will make them smooth. Nothing now remains but to fasten the work together. There are several methods of doing this.

Either small brads or screws can be used, or if the design is small, glue alone will answer. Brads are objectionable in all small brackets or thin woods, as the work is liable to break while driving them in. Where the bracket is intended for use and to carry some weight, the shelf and support should be fastened with screws. To do this, mark the points where screws are to go and drill holes in the back of bracket large enough for the screws to pass through easily. Then apply the support and mark points exactly corresponding to the holes in the bracket. A small hole should be made in the support at these points to start the screw. Then put in the screws and fasten the work together. Before making these holes in the bracket the design should be examined to see that the screws will enter the support at a place where the wood is thick enough. In the design before us the points marked Z would be the proper places for the screws.

For small brackets, glue alone will be sufficient, and instructions for using glue will be found in the chapter on that subject.

In making a large bracket, small brass hinges can be used to advantage in fastening the support and shelf, so that they can be shut up for transportation.

CHAPTER VI.

MAKING AN EASEL

AN easel generally consists of three parts — the upright, the leg and the shelf. Take the pattern shown in plate II, and prepare the wood as before described. The several parts are to be cut out in the same way as the bracket In cutting the veins in the leaves, a very small hole should be drilled near where the stem joins, and the veins sawed with a fine saw. In case a leaf has no other support than its stem, to avoid breaking, the veins should be cut before the outside of the leaf. If the wood is holly, or of a light color and close grain, a very pretty effect will be produced by marking the veins, and also the outside of the leaf (where it lays upon other parts of the design), with India ink The veins shown in the design are for sawing only; in case India ink is used, other and more delicate veins can be added with the pen, as in one lower leaf.

Having cut out all the parts, smoothed the surface and edges, the shelf can be fastened in its proper place with glue. In this design the shelf is simply a straight piece of wood, four and one-half inches long by three-fourths wide, and is to have a peg at each end to hold a book open or keep a picture in its place.

Now comes the leg, in fastening which to the upright considerable difficulty is frequently experienced. These are the best

AN EASEL.

ways: Take a hinge, and with small screws fasten one part to the end of the leg first; then lay the leg on the back of the upright, and when the hinge is in the right position (which can be ascertained by holding it in place with the fingers and trying it to see if the easel stands square) mark the spots for the screw holes and put in the screws.

The following cut will show this more plainly:

Notice the direction of the screws.

Another good way is to cut two pieces of one-eighth wood in this shape:

Drill a small hole in them, about one-fourth of an inch from the flat side. Glue these to the back of the easel, far enough apart to let the leg go between them. Then drill a hole in the leg about one-fourth inch from the end, place the leg between the two ears, and pass a wire or round peg of hard wood through the holes. This mode of fastening the leg will be found advantageous when the wood is too thin for screws.

CHAPTER VII.

SANDPAPER

IT would seem as if sandpapering were one of the easiest and simplest matters, and yet there are few things connected with this art that are so little understood. The ordinary way with the novice is to tear off a piece of sandpaper, hold it with his fingers, and rub the wood with it. This method is very likely to lead to bad results. If it is a piece of open work that needs smoothing the paper takes off too much wood at the edges, and rounds them off. Or, if it is a flat piece of wood, the fingers bear on harder in some places than others, and make the surface uneven.

Now, there are two ways to sandpaper nicely. If the piece of work is small, like the bracket before described, for instance, fasten a whole sheet of sandpaper to your bench or a flat, smooth board, and rub the wood over it. This is the best method for all small articles. For general purposes, however, it is best to make a sand-board, which is done in this way: Cut two pieces of smooth pine, three-eighths of an inch thick, three inches wide and four long; through one of them put three slender screws in a line and one and one-half inches apart, long enough when the heads are driven in flush with the wood to have the points project about one-fourth inch on the other side.

SANDPAPER.

File these points sharp, and make corresponding holes in the other block. Now cut a piece of sandpaper four inches wide and seven and one-half long, and lay one end upon the screw points, pressing them through the paper. Then stretch the paper tightly around the block, and fasten the other end upon the points. Lay upon this the other block, and fasten the two together with a screw at each end. A pair of common screw-eyes that are used for hanging picture frames will be useful for this purpose. It would be well to have two sets of these blocks made to hold coarse and fine sandpaper. Now lay the work upon the bench, hold it with one hand and rub with the sand-board, carefully and briskly, and with a circular motion. If the wood is at all rough, begin with No. 1 sandpaper, and finish with No. 00. Before using the paper on any fine work examine it carefully, and pick out any large pieces of sand which might score the wood.

If the amateur is fortunate enough to possess a turning-lathe he will find that the following contrivance will save him a great deal of labor: Make (or have them made by some turner) several cylinders of wood, four inches long and three and one-half in diameter. Stretch around one of these a half sheet of sandpaper, and glue the two ends to the wood. Set this in the lathe, revolve rapidly, and it will smooth the wood very quickly. The writer uses half a dozen of these cylinders, with a different number of sandpaper on each.

CHAPTER VIII.

GLUE, SHELLAC, OIL AND POLISH

NO amateur can have a complete outfit without a glue-pot; indeed, no family should be without one, and every one should know how to use it. The use of glue, however, is little understood, and it is too often found that articles carelessly glued together do not adhere firmly. A careful attention to the ensuing remarks will enable anyone to make solid joints. The glue-pot should be double,— one pot within another. They are for sale at all hardware stores, and cost all the way from fifty cents up. The outer pot is to be partly filled with water, the inner one contains the glue. The ordinary white glue is the strongest, and should be broken into small pieces. Put these in the pot and cover them with cold water. Then place the pot upon the stove, and let the water boil. This will soon dissolve the glue, which should be of the consistency of thin cream. If it is too thick, add more water and let it boil a little longer; if too thin, add a little more glue. Have a small brush to apply it to the wood. Do not use a stick for this purpose, as many do, but have a brush. Warm the wood, and *always remember that the glue must be applied hot*. If it is allowed to cool, though still liquid, it will not make a strong joint. Press the parts together, so as to squeeze out all the glue possible. If the wood is of a shape that admits of it, clamp the pieces stoutly together and let them stand for several hours. If clamps cannot be used, bind the parts together with cord, or lay weights upon them.

Turn back now to the small bracket, and see how the support should be glued to the main part. Drill two or three holes at the points Z, and make corresponding holes in the edge of the support. Cut short pegs and put them in the holes. These will serve to hold the parts in their place till the glue has set. Now warm the edge of the support, apply the glue, and join the parts together, the pegs in the support entering the holes in the bracket. Then lay the bracket on a table, have some small sticks about a foot long, put the ends from opposite sides in the open spaces of the support, letting the other ends rest on the table, and on these sticks lay a book or some other weight. In this way the two parts will be held firmly together till the glue hardens. To glue on the shelf apply the glue to the edge of the back and support, lay the whole on a sheet of paper on the table, put on the shelf, and hold it in its position by placing a heavy weight against it on one side while other weights are laid on the bracket.

SHELLAC

A very fair finish can be put upon most close-grained woods by simply using shellac. To prepare it, take a small bottle of alcohol, and fill it about one-quarter full of bleached shellac (for sale at all drug stores) broken into small pieces, which will be dissolved after standing several hours. It can be rubbed on the wood with a small piece of sponge or wad of cotton. It dries almost immediately, so that several coats can be applied in a few minutes.

White holly is very much improved and rendered less liable to soil and catch dirt if it be given a coat of shellac and afterward rubbed down with very fine sandpaper. Where it is desired to use India ink on holly for marking veins of leaves, as in the case of the easel before described, to prevent the ink spreading the wood should have one or two coats of shellac, and afterward be rubbed down very smooth as above. The shellac fills up the pores of the wood.

OIL

A very good dead finish can be given to black walnut by rubbing on it boiled linseed oil, and, after this has been absorbed, rubbing it down with soft paper. One or two coats of shellac afterward applied will give the wood a very fair polish.

FRENCH POLISHING

This is by far the finest way for finishing woods, but requires care and patience. Prepared French polish is generally for sale at paint stores, or wherever they keep artists' materials, or supplies for amateur scroll-sawing. A small bottle of McIntyre's London Polish, or any other good polish, will be sufficient for the wants of most amateurs. If the amateur cannot find it in his own town, and desires a large quantity of it, the following recipe will answer: Into a pint bottle of alcohol put one quarter ounce of gum copal, one quarter ounce of gum arabic and one ounce shellac, all ground fine; cork the bottle tight, and let it stand in a warm place near a stove, and be shaken occasionally. After two or three days the gums will be nearly dissolved. Then strain through a piece of muslin, and keep corked for use.

Now for its application. In the first place, the wood must be smooth. Use the finest sandpaper, and be careful to take out every scratch, which will be sure to show badly after polishing. When the wood is thus prepared, if it is a close-grained wood, such as holly or satin, give it a coat of shellac, and smooth this off with the sandpaper. Then take a small wad of cotton wool, pour a little polish on it, and rub over the wood. This first coat will be absorbed, and after it dries pour a little more polish on the wad, wrap this in a piece of soft linen or cotton, apply to the outside a drop or two of either raw linseed oil or sweet oil, and rub the wood briskly with a circular motion. If the wad gets sticky, apply a little more oil. After a few minutes' rubbing let the wood stand a little while to dry, and then go over it again with polish and oil, repeating this process several times. Avoid using too much polish, or it may take off the polish previously applied. For the last one or two coats it is better to use a thinner polish made by mixing one part of the polish with two parts of alcohol. After a little experience, and one or two failures, the amateur will be able to polish beautifully.

Where the wood is of an open grain, such as walnut, cedar, maple, etc, it is necessary after smoothing them to rub them down with a coat of light or dark filling, according to the color of the woods. This filling can be obtained at nearly all places where the polish is kept. The filling should dry about twenty minutes, then be rubbed off with a cloth or soft paper, and the wood sandpapered smooth. After this put on a coat of shellac, sandpaper smooth and apply polish as before.

Where brackets or any open-work pieces are to be polished, it should be done before the sawing; otherwise, in rubbing the work, small pieces are liable to be broken off, and the polish will stain the edges of the wood

As polishing is a tedious process, amateurs can save themselves some trouble by sending their work to a polisher, who can be found wherever fine furniture is manufactured.

CHAPTER IX.

GLUED VENEERS

IN fret-work articles a very pretty effect can be produced by using what are called glued veneers. These can be obtained of dealers in sawing materials, costing from fifty to seventy-five cents per square foot. They are made either of two veneers glued on the front and back of some cheap wood, such as poplar or walnut, or three veneers glued together. As the amateur may frequently want a combination of veneers of different colors to those usually sold, he should know how to arrange them for himself. A popular kind is to have holly outside, with black inside. Cut two pieces of holly of the required size and one piece of black, with its grain running at right angles to that of the holly. Have two blocks of smooth, flat wood, about a foot square, or larger, and some strong clamp-screws, either wooden or iron. Warm the veneers, make the glue rather thin, apply it freely to one piece of the holly, and lay the black upon this. Then put glue on the other piece of holly, place this upon the black and clamp the whole very tightly together between the blocks, having a sheet of paper next to the blocks to prevent the surplus glue from adhering to them. They should be kept under pressure till the glue has thoroughly hardened. Then they can be removed and the outsides smoothed for use with sandpaper. It is necessary to have three veneers to prevent warping. This way of arranging woods will be found of great advantage when one has to saw out any very delicate work, as the inner piece of wood, having its grain cross the others, makes the whole very strong and less liable to break.

CHAPTER X.

OVERLAYING.

WHEN the amateur has mastered his saw, so that he can cut out intricate patterns easily, he should commence overlaying. At a picture dealer's procure a flat frame, from one and one-half to two or three inches in width, of either gilt or polished natural or dyed wood. Saw out a border of tracery or scroll work of one-sixteenth wood (previously polished) and fasten it to the frame with gilt or silver escutcheon pins. The effect will be very beautiful if the work is carefully done. Designs for this class of work can be purchased of all dealers. Very pretty patterns can often be found stamped in the covers of books.

At the end of this book will be found two designs for overlaid frames, the one with oak leaves in the corners, and the wreath of ivy leaves. The main parts can be made of either polished wood or velvet. To prepare the latter, cut out a piece of one-eighth pine with the oval in center, and cut a piece of velvet about half an inch larger each way. Glue the velvet upon one side of the wood, cut a V-shaped piece out of each corner of the velvet, fold the edges over and glue to the other side. When it is dry, cut the oval out of the velvet a little smaller than the wood, and turn this edge in so that from the front nothing but velvet shows. Then glue to the back three strips of wood one-quarter inch wide, placing them about an inch from the sides and bottom, and to these strips glue a piece of pine to hold the picture. If this is then covered with bookbinders' muslin the back will be complete.

The wreath of ivy leaves, for instance, having been sawed, of one-sixteenth wood or veneer, lay it upon the velvet, and when adjusted to the proper place, stick two or three pins into the velvet through the spaces between the stems. Then remove the wreath, apply a touch of glue to the center of each leaf, being careful to do this to the right side, and lay it again on the velvet, the pins guiding it to the proper place. Remove the pins, place a light weight upon the wreath till the glue has hardened, and the frame is done.

If the wreath is to be put upon a polished surface in place of the velvet, it will be necessary to secure it with escutcheon pins, or to scratch off a little of the polish under each leaf to make the glue adhere.

Brackets or frames of plain design will be very much improved by overlaying on them a leaf or cluster of leaves, or a head or any other ornament, cut out of another kind of wood.

CHAPTER XI

INLAYING

THIS is the most beautiful part of scroll-sawing, and should be well understood by every amateur. At first thought it may strike the beginner that, in order to inlay one piece of wood in another, it is necessary first to cut out the pattern from the one and afterward very carefully to cut the same pattern a trifle smaller from a different wood, and fit it into the former piece. Inlaying could be done in this way, but it would be attended with considerable difficulty, as in both cases the pattern would need to be followed with great nicety. There is a far simpler way than this, and it consists in *sawing the design out of two woods at the same time.*

For example, take the design of the paper-knife with an oak leaf in the handle. Suppose we wish to make the knife of walnut and inlay with a satinwood leaf. Take a piece of walnut one and one-half inches wide and nine inches long, and cut a piece of satin the same size; fasten the two together with a brad in each corner; trace the design upon the satin,—or paste it on,—and with a very fine drill, which should be as small as a pin, if possible, make a hole through both woods at the lower end of the vein. Use a No. 0 saw blade, and cut all the veins. Then drill another small hole at the end of the short twig, and with a very fine saw blade, No. 000, proceed to cut out the leaf and acorn. In doing this care must be taken to keep on the line. The fine blade will turn the sharpest corner. If the saw gets off the line keep right on and get back to the line as soon as possible, as this will not prevent the woods inlaying, though it may mar the beauty of the figure. Saw all the way around the leaf and twig and acorn to the place of starting, and the leaves will drop out. Then the little figure in the blade of the knife can be cut out in the same manner, if it is desired to inlay that part, or it can be left as an open space. Now cut out the outside of the knife, and the work of the saw will have been done. Get the glue-pot ready, take the walnut knife, and lay the glue around the inside edges of the leaf opening. Insert quickly in this the satin leaf, lay the whole upon a piece of paper on the table, and with the brush work some glue into the veins, and also lay a little more glue along the edges of the inlay. Place the handle of the knife between two blocks of wood, with paper on each side to prevent the glue adhering to them, and clamp them tightly together. The pressure will force the surplus glue into the veins, and will fill all the space around the edge. The walnut leaf can then be glued into the satin knife in the same way. After the glue has had time to harden, which should take half a day, the paper can be removed by slightly moistening and scraping it, and the surface of the handle smoothed off with file and sandpaper. If, after this is done, some small holes are noticed in the edge or veins of the leaf, they can be filled with a touch of glue. This will harden in a short time, and after making the blade of the knife sharp with file and sandpaper, the handle can again be smoothed and polished if desired. The result is two paper-knives, one of walnut inlaid with satin leaf, the other of satin with a walnut leaf. Notice that when a light wood is inlaid in a dark wood, or *vice versa*, the cut made by the saw hardly shows, as it is filled with glue which is nearly the color of the darker wood. It sometimes happens that no fine drill is at hand to make the hole for the saw. If a coarse drill is used, or if a small piece of the inlay should be broken off and lost, it will be necessary to fit another piece of wood into the hole, or fill it with a mixture of glue and sawdust.

INLAYING VENEERS

Now take the ivy-leaf paper-knife and inlay with veneers. And for this it is supposed that the amateur has a first-class treadle machine, which will run perfectly true and carry the finest saws. Cut six or eight pieces of colored veneers, some green, red, black, white, etc., each two by nine inches. Cut also two pieces of one-sixteenth wood the above size, one of holly and one of walnut. Place the veneers between these and fasten together by gluing the edges. These thicker pieces of wood are used to strengthen the veneers while sawing, and to prevent breaking off any delicate portions. Apply the design and saw the veins as described above; then drill a fine hole at one end of the vine, and saw along the vine to the point where it is covered by the leaf, then along the edge of leaf and back along the other side of vine to starting point. The six or eight stems will drop out, and can be placed in a box or by themselves, with some mark on them and a corresponding mark on the pattern, so that it will be known where the pieces belong. A portion of the vine being thus removed, the leaves immediately joining it can be cut out, making one piece of the leaf and its stem. The remainder of the design can be sawed in the same way, and in doing this it will be noticed that it has been necessary to drill but one hole for the saw aside from those made for cutting the veins. After cutting out the leaves and vine, the woods can be separated with a knife-blade. Never mind the outside of the paper-knife at present, that will be shaped hereafter.

Now take one of the pieces, the black, for example, and lay it on a sheet of paper on the table. Pick out the green leaves and lay them in the proper places (no glue to be used at present), and lay in also a white vine, and the little pieces of black that go between the stems and the vine. When these are all in place, take a strip of paper, the size of the black wood, smear it with mucilage or paste, place it upon the inlay, and keep a weight upon it until dry. Then take the other woods and put in the leaves and vines of the different colors, and paste on the paper in the same way as above. For the two pieces of one sixteenth wood glue the holly leaves and vine into the walnut, and *vice versa*, as described in making the oak-leaf paper-knives, and when the glue has hardened, scrape off the paper, smooth them, fill the holes if necessary, and shape the outside.

Now to make paper-knives out of the veneers. If there are six of them they will make three knives. Cut three strips of one-sixteenth holly the size of the veneer. These are for the centers, and to have an inlay glued to each side. The strips of paper pasted on the veneers were to hold the leaves in their places till they were ready for use. Have the glue ready, smear it freely on both sides of the holly, and apply a veneer on each side, with the paper outside; then clamp them tightly together, being careful that the veneers do not slide out of position. When dry, scrape off the paper, fill the lines with glue where needed, and when this has dried, sandpaper smooth, shape the outside as in the design, sharpen the edges with file and sandpaper, and then polish the whole; and behold a very pretty paper-knife, the two sides of different colors.

After these two examples have been carefully done the amateur can attempt more intricate pieces, and will have little difficulty.

SHADING

It is frequently desirable to shade different parts of inlaid woods, to give them a rounded appearance, and this is done in a very simple manner.

Take a small iron pot or pan, partly filled with dry, fine sand, and place it upon the fire. When the sand is well heated, press into it a piece of light wood, and notice how the wood is browned. If pressed too deep or held too long in the sand, the lower edge will be charred, therefore, it is necessary to keep withdrawing the wood, so as not to scorch too much, and to watch the effect. A few experiments on waste wood in this way will familiarize the amateur with the process and enable him to do some very good shading. Holly and maple, and other light woods, can be used for this purpose. In shading inlays care must be taken to use only perfectly dry woods, as the scorching may so shrink the woods that they will not fit in their places. It would be well, therefore, to dry or bake the woods well before sawing.

SAWING ON A BEVEL.

There is another way to inlay, by sawing the woods on a bevel. For instance, take two pieces of dark and two of light wood, and tack them together as in the illustration below.

The piece cut out of No. 1 will fit close in No. 2, and that from No. 3 in No. 4; also, the light piece from No. 2 will fit in No. 3. To saw in this way, when using the hand-saw, the wooden rest can be easily inclined to the proper angle, while the saw itself is to be worked perpendicularly, as in ordinary sawing. Some of the treadle machines have beveling attachments made for this kind of work. The amateur will find, however, that the manner of inlaying first described will answer for all ordinary purposes.

A JEWEL BOX.

A very pretty way in which to use inlays is to glue them to the tops of small wooden boxes, such as jewel boxes and the like. The inlay is to be prepared in the same way as those for the ivy-leaf paper-knife, the veneer being cut somewhat larger than the top of the box. It is then to be glued to the cover, and at the same time a veneer must be glued on the inside, to prevent the cover from warping. Afterward the edges can be filed off flush with the sides of the box, or rounded, as desired, and the top polished.

CHAPTER XII.

SILHOUETTES.

THERE are few articles made with the scroll-saw prettier or more ornamental than silhouettes. Sheets of these designs are generally for sale at book stores and by dealers in sawing materials, and cost from fifteen to twenty-five cents per sheet. Many beautiful designs can also be found in books illustrated by Konewka and other artists, and frequently in books for children. The following design will serve for an example:

This can be cut from ebony, either one-sixteenth of an inch thick, or any other close grained wood of that thickness, or from veneers. The various colors of dyed veneers will be found very useful for making silhouettes. The wood must be made perfectly smooth before tracing the pattern. It is essential in this class of work, as well as for inlaying, to use only the finest quality of saw blades, those with perfect and regular teeth. A No. 0 or 1 blade should be used, except for the most delicate parts, such as the lips, hair, eyelashes, etc., which require a No. 000. Where veneers are used, they should be held or glued between two thicker woods to prevent them breaking.

Silhouettes are used in a variety of ways, either by overlaying on a sheet of polished wood, or by mounting them on a piece of moulding, with a slit sawed in it lengthwise.

If the amateur has a first-class treadle machine, he can easily decorate the walls of a room by applying silhouettes in the following manner. Procure a quantity of some cheap veneer, such as walnut or holly or rosewood, and cut into strips about six inches wide, and square at the ends. Sandpaper them smooth, and finish with shellac or polish. Then select a number of designs, the more the better, and saw half-a-dozen or more of each. Glue these, at regular intervals, and on a line, to the strips of veneer. These can then be tacked to the wall, all the way around the room, a few inches below the ceiling. By a tasteful selection of designs, and careful fitting of the strips, one can in this way beautify his home at a trifling expense.

SILHOUETTE LIKENESSES.

The following is an ingenious way for cutting silhouette likenesses of children and others for overlaying. With a strong light throw the shadow of the child's head (in profile) on a sheet of paper tacked against the wall. Quickly trace the features, shape of head, etc, with a pencil. A little practice will enable any one to make admirable likenesses in this way. Then, with a pentagraph — an instrument for reducing or enlarging drawings, for sale generally wherever artists' materials are kept, from one dollar up — make a reduced sketch of the head, as small as desired. This can then be applied to the wood, and cut out in silhouette as before described. In this simple way any one can decorate an easel or bracket, or any other article of fretwork, with an accurate profile likeness of some friend.

CHAPTER XIII.

DESCRIPTION OF DESIGNS

PLATE I

FIGURE 1. Design for bracket, fully described in Chapter V.
Figure 2 Design for card basket. This can be made from one-sixteenth holly, satin or walnut, or from one-eighth wood If of holly or other light-colored wood, the veins in the leaves can be traced with a fine pen in India ink; also the edges of the leaves, where they overlap each other or the border of design. For a square card basket, cut out four sides, and a base two and three-fourths inches square; drill holes where marked, and tie the whole together with silk thread or narrow ribbon.

PLATE II.

Design for an easel as described in Chapter VI.

PLATE III.

Design for a card picture frame. The ivy-leaf can be either

overlaid or inlaid. For overlaying, use either veneers or one-sixteenth woods.

PLATE IV.

Three designs for paper-knives; two for inlaying and one for open work. Any other letters can easily be substituted for those in pattern.

PLATE V.

Design for a card picture frame, either for inlaying or overlaying.

PLATE VI.

Design for a card picture frame. The back, to hold the picture can be made as described in Chapter X, and the veins in leaves either traced in India ink or cut with saw.

PLATE VII.

Design for end of bookstand. Cut from polished wood, either one-eighth or three-sixteenths of an inch thick. Make two of them. Then take two pieces of one-quarter or three-eighths wood, the upper one four and five-eighths, and lower one five and a half inches wide, and as long as desired. Fasten the ends of bookstand to these with round-headed screws. Ordinary countersunk screws should not be used, as they might split the wood in driving tight

If the above pieces of wood are cut thirteen inches long the bookstand will be just the right size to hold the sixteen volumes of the "Little Classics." A small silhouette should be glued to the center of the shield before the stand is put together. A bookstand made in this style will be found very convenient, as the top makes a nice shelf for standing various articles.

PLATE VIII.

Design for a card picture frame, similar to Plate VI, but with a different style of ivy-leaf.

PLATE IX.

Design for a shrine card frame. This can be cut from one-sixteenth or one-eighth wood. The two doors or gates are to be fastened on with hinges. For this rustic and pretty pattern the author is indebted to Mr Chris. Arnold, of Chicago, a designer and scroll sawyer of considerable merit.

PLATES X TO XIV.

Various silhouettes.

PLATES XV AND XVI.

Initial letters.

To use these designs, take a sheet of thin letter copying-paper, place it upon the pattern and trace the lines with a sharp lead pencil. After this is done, paste this thin paper on a sheet of white paper or card and apply to the wood as heretofore described. The copying-paper needs to be pasted on white paper to make the pencil marks more distinct.

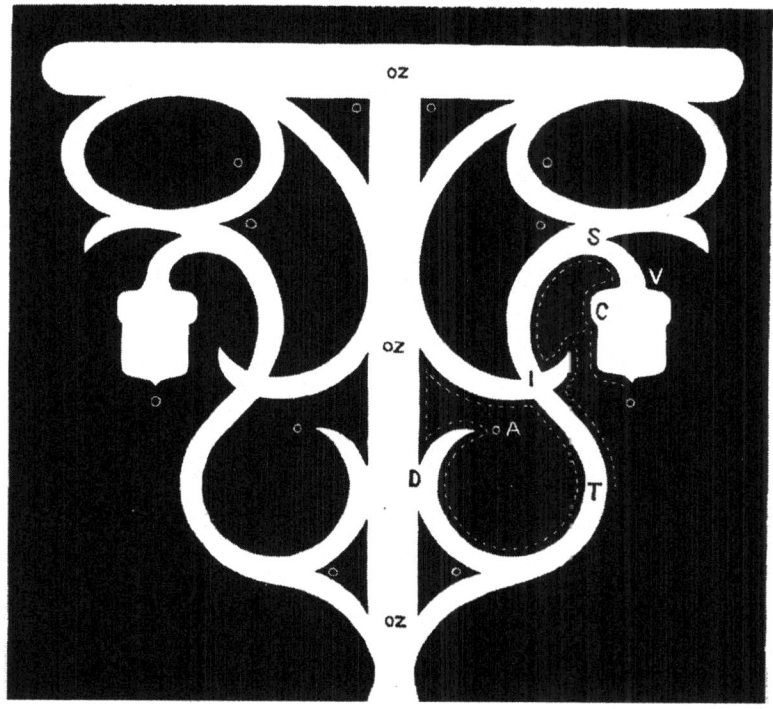

PLATE III.

PLATE V.

PLATE VI.

PLATE VII

PLATE VIII.

PLATE IX.

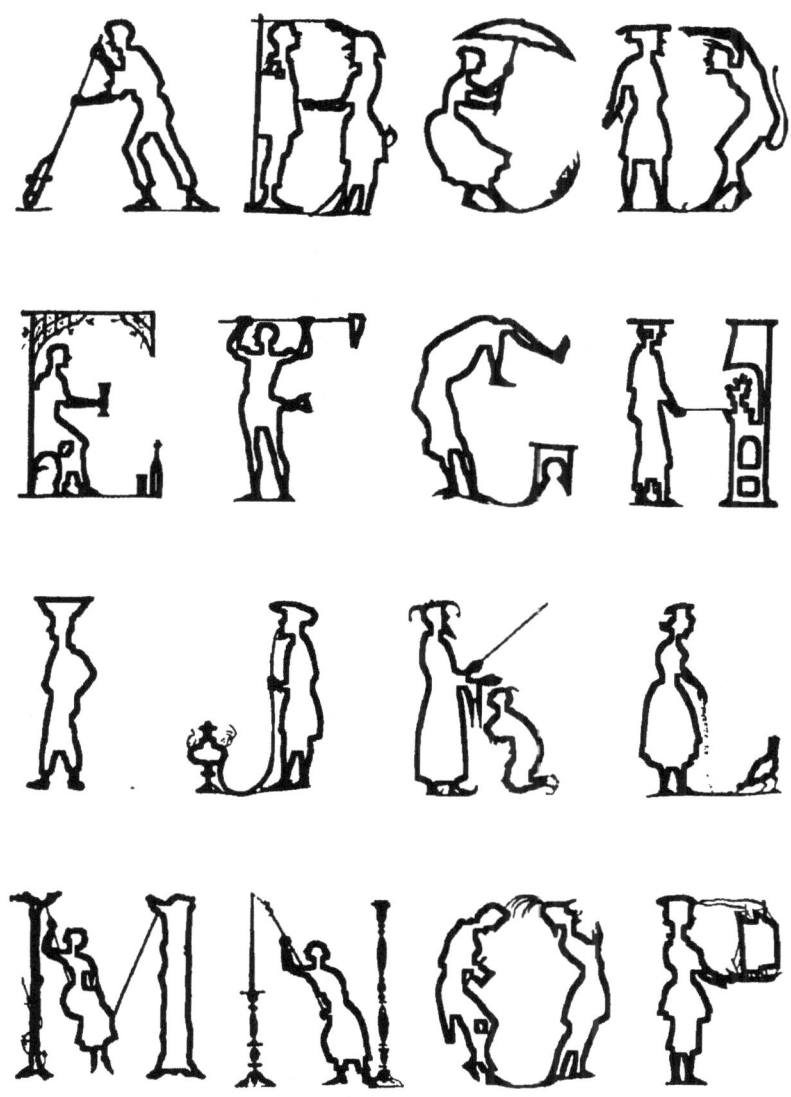

ADVERTISEMENTS.

THE CENTENNIAL PRIZE MEDAL
THE ONLY ONE AWARDED FOR
FOOT-POWER SAWS,
GIVEN TO
TRUMP BROS.
WILMINGTON, DEL.

THE
FLEETWOOD SCROLL SAW
For all descriptions of light Scroll or Fret Sawing in

Wood, Bone, Ivory, Shell or Metal.
ITS ADVANTAGES ARE
SIMPLICITY of Construction.
STRENGTH of all the parts.
COMPACT and GRACEFUL Form.
QUIET MOVEMENT and the
LOW PRICE at which it is sold.

5,000 of these Machines have been sold to Amateurs, Jewelers, Model Makers, Shell Workers, Printers, Ladies, Boys and Girls.

Brackets, Easels, Picture Frames, Boxes, Table Mats,
ETC. ETC., IN OPEN SCROLL,
INLAID OR MOSAIC WORK.

For RAPIDITY, PRECISION, EASE OF WORKING, DURABILITY and SUPERIOR FINISH, these Machines are not equaled.

Price $13 to $25.

For artistic work and delicate cutting, especially INLAYING or MOSAIC OVERLAYING and the cutting of SILHOUETTES, the FLEETWOOD surpasses all others. Indeed, it is the only Machine that will retain that delicacy of cutting and expression which are essential in artistic work. This feature in the FLEETWOOD is attained by careful workmanship, good material, and the general design of the Machine, which is based upon true mechanical principles.

The Machines are warranted in all respects as represented. Each one is carefully tried before leaving the factory, and if not right in every particular is not sent out.

Amateur Wood Workers

FURNISHED WITH ALL THE

CHOICE AND FANCY WOODS,

Planed and unplaned, of any thickness, from one-sixteenth of an inch up, and in any quantity down to a single board. The following is a list of the principal kinds constantly on hand

BLACK WALNUT	WHITE HOLLY	ROSEWOOD
MAHOGANY,	SATINWOOD	HUNGARIAN ASH,
WHITE ASH,	AMARANTH,	THUYA,
TULIP,	EBONY,	COCOBALO,
CALIFORNIA ROSEWOOD	BIRDSEYE MAPLE,	CURLED MAPLE,
BUTTERNUT,	OAK	CHERRY,
POPLAR	RED CEDAR,	WHITE CEDAR,
SPANISH CEDAR,	ETC ETC	ETC, ETC

Enclose 3-cent stamp for Catalogue and Price List, in which full particulars are given to assist parties in making out their orders

WHOLESALE DEALERS

Are directed to our General Price List, and their attention solicited to our large and attractive stock of

Hard Wood Lumber and Veneers,

Which for Quality, Quantity, and Inducement of Prices, merits the consideration of close buyers

SPANISH AND WHITE CEDAR.
RACING BOAT STOCK, EXTRA LENGTH AND QUALITY.

GEORGE W. READ & CO.

STEAM BAND SAW AND VENEER MILL,

Nos. 186 to 200 Lewis Street,

Foot of Fifth to Sixth Street, E R   NEW YORK.

THE
DEXTER MACHINE,
PATENTED OCTOBER, 1876,

A Light-Running, Rapid-Cutting Machine Thoroughly Made and Very Durable.

Price, with Half-dozen Saws, $6.00.

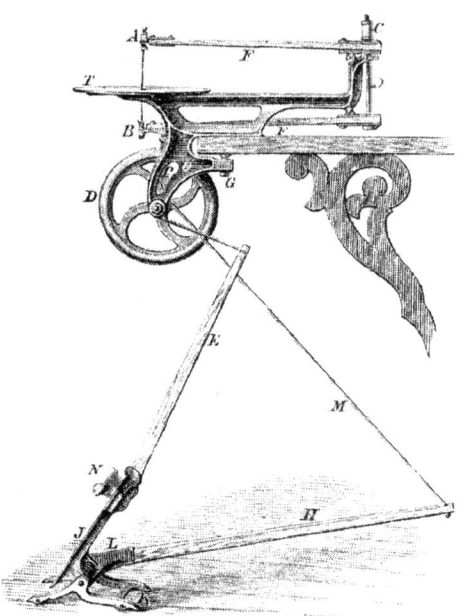

SEND FOR DESCRIPTIVE CIRCULAR AND ILLUSTRATED LIST OF DESIGNS.

TRUMP BROS.

Wilmington, Del.

FIRST-CLASS WORK AT FAIR PRICES.

BAKER & CO.
DESIGNERS AND
ENGRAVERS ON WOOD
FOOT BLOCK, COR. OF CLARK & MONROE STS.
CHICAGO.
DEALERS IN ENGRAVING TOOLS AND ENGRAVERS SUPPLIES.

DRAWING INSTRUMENTS, PANTOGRAPHS
AND ENGRAVER'S OUTFITS.

All Kinds of Engraving Tools.

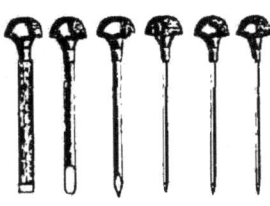

PRINTER'S SET.
Six Tools, ready for use, $2.50.

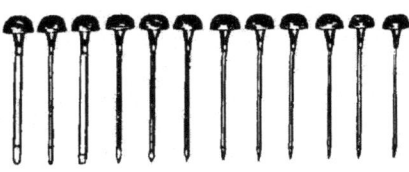

AMATEUR'S SET.
Twelve Tools, ready for use, $5.00.

SEND STAMP FOR PRICE LIST.

ST. LOUIS SAW WORKS
Established in 1849.

BRANCH, CROOKES & CO.
MANUFACTURERS

224 Lake Street,   80 Carondelet St.
CHICAGO.   **NEW ORLEANS.**

114 & 116 Vine St.
ST. LOUIS.

A full stock of all kinds of Saws, Saw Gummers, Emery Wheels, Mill and Taper Files, Perin's French Band Saw Blades, Knickerbocker Ice Tools. Repairing promptly attended to.
Send for Catalogue of Prices.

BRANCH, CROOKES & CO.
223 Lake St., cor. of Franklin, Chicago.

BUY THE IMPROVED

HOME
SHUTTLE
Sewing Machine.
PRICE $40.

It has no superior as a First-Class Lock-Stitch Sewing Machine. IT IS THE CHEAPEST IN THE WORLD. Large discounts for cash.

AGENTS WANTED EVERYWHERE.

Machines sent on trial to any part of the country at our expense if not accepted. Send for latest circulars and terms to cash purchasers, or call and examine when in the city.

JOHNSON, CLARK & CO., Manufacturers,
No. 141 State Street, Chicago.

Send for circular, and be sure and say where you saw this card.